Planes of the Presidents

Bill Holder

Schiffer Military History
Atglen, PA

Acknolwedgments

1. Stephanie Mitchell, The Arizona Aerospace Foundation
2. Mike Tull, Charles Ramey and Lori May, Boeing Communications
3. Linda Delatorre, Johnson Controls, World Services
4. Sgt. Dan Neely, 89th Airlift Wing, Andrews AFB, MD
5. HMX-1 Marine Helicopter Squadron, Quantico, VA

Book Design by Ian Robertson.

Printed in China.
ISBN: 0-7643-1187-5

We are interested in hearing from authors with book ideas on related topics.

Published by Schiffer Publishing Ltd.
4880 Lower Valley Road
Atglen, PA 19310
Phone: (610) 593-1777
FAX: (610) 593-2002
E-mail: Schifferbk@aol.com.
Visit our web site at: www.schifferbooks.com
Please write for a free catalog.
This book may be purchased from the publisher.
Please include $3.95 postage.
Try your bookstore first.

In Europe, Schiffer books are distributed by:
Bushwood Books
6 Marksbury Avenue
Kew Gardens
Surrey TW9 4JF
England
Phone: 44 (0)208 392-8585
FAX: 44 (0)208 392-9876
E-mail: Bushwd@aol.com.
Free postage in the UK. Europe: air mail at cost.
Try your bookstore first.

Contents

1

Introduction

"You have been cleared to land," crackles the control tower radio to a Boeing 747 on final approach. A commerical airliner like hundreds of others flying everyday? Nope, this 747 flight is quite unique.

As this giant swept-wing, wide-body transport breaks through the clouds, you do not see a TWA or Delta insignia on its side, but instead the words "United States of America" painted on its fuselage. Then, there are also that Presidential Seal near the main entry door and the American Flag on the tail that really catch your attention.

The huge plane, in the hands of a highly-skilled military pilot, glides in like a dove for a perfect landing. What you have witnessed is a familiar sight at Andrews Air Force Base, Maryland, that being the landing of the current presidential aircraft, Air Force One.

The Boeing 747 is the latest in a fairly long line of presidential aircraft throughout the years. But be assured, it is certainly the largest and most complex of any of the planes that have gone before. It might be surprising to learn that American presidents have been flying in their own designated planes since the 1940s. A far cry from today's versions, a number of the initial versions possessed few, if any, changes to the commercial or military transport that was used for the important mission.

The commercial airlines provided the first presidential planes, a Pan American Clipper, to be exact. FDR also flew aboard a standard C-54 which was piloted by a TWA crew.

Some of the planes in this unique fleet through the years have received official names, while others picked up unofficial monikers from the press and crew members, some of which stuck like glue to the planes.

Modern-era presidents have used the presidential plane to great advantage as they have conducted world-wide business and the attending of official functions. For example, President Reagan visited 26 different countries and territories during his eight year tenure. President Bush bested that figure in just four years with visits to 36 countries. But President Clinton was by far the greatest user of the official means of transportation with 59 trips during the first seven years of his administration.

Everything that could be done to the earlier presidential aircraft was attempted in order to make them as inconspicuous as possible. They certainly did not want to identify the plane as that transporting the American president.

A view of a number of the presidential aircraft fleet at the Air Force Museum at Wright Patterson AFB. (Holder Photo)

The Columbine II was one of a number of Lockheed Constellations that served as presidential aircraft. (USAF Photo)

The Independence, a modified C-118, was one of the first presidential aircraft to be specially painted to dignify it with its special mission. (USAF Photo)

That, of course, certainly is not the situation with the modern presidential planes, which are detailed to the hilt, making them a real aerial showpiece and certainly a pride to this country.

Since the days of WWII, air transportation for the president has come a long way from the day a presidential flight made front page news. Today, a presidential flight is as common as a ride in his limousine, and probably much safer.

In the next few decades we will see even more changes in transporting the president. Someday, there may even be a supersonic transport with a Presidential Seal on its fuselage. And perhaps in the more distant future, a special space shuttle-type vehicle might be ready to take the Chief Executive into orbit to visit a space station.

The plane that most recognize as Air Force One, a modified Boeing 707, that carried the now-familiar blue and white paint scheme. (USAF Photo)

A view of President Kennedy and party emerging from the 26000 presidential aircraft. (USAF Photo)

The latest presidential aircraft, a model based on the Boeing 747, is shown during a take-off during its flight test program. (Boeing Photo)

The magnificent 747 Air Force One will serve as a symbol of the United States for many decades to come. (Boeing Photo)

2
The Early Ones

Noting the routine professionalism which accompanies the flying of such an important cargo as the President of the United States makes you wonder, has it always been that way? Not really!

When presidents first started taking to the air back during WWII, many feared for their safety. That was particularly the case with FDR, who was in the air when the war was still going hot and heavy. But in recent decades, flying has become a way of life for the president, who can, and has, circled the globe at a moment's notice.

It might be surprising to learn that presidential aircraft stretch back to the 1930s. But the first presidential flight, although not an official one, was when President Teddy Roosevelt was a passenger in a Wright B Flyer. It must be noted that the flight took place after his presidential term was completed. But even so, it was a significant first.

Following are the planes that served in early presidential transportation:

Curtiss YC-30 Condor

Although never confirmed, there is some data pointing to the possibility of the existence of a presidential aircraft in the 1935 time period. If true, it would have to be considered the first presidential aircraft. The plane was a bi-wing twin-engine transport known as the YC-30 Condor.

The Condor was a significant performer, with a maximum payload capability of about 4,000 pounds which equated to about a 15-passenger capability. It was powered by a pair of Wright 1820-23 engines, each producing 720 horsepower.

It was reported that one of these planes had been modified with comfortable chairs, a couch, and other niceties that would point to its possible presidential-transporting duties.

Several of these planes were reportedly located at Bolling Field, just outside of Washington, DC, which would certainly have been the correct location for such an aircraft. There is no solid data to support this proposition, but it could certainly be possible.

A view of a Wright B Flyer in flight, a plane that served to transport President Teddy Roosevelt in 1911. (Wright State University Photo)

An early photo showing a Wright B Flyer. This plane could be unofficially called the first presidential aircraft. (Wright State University Photo)

Although never officially confirmed, there is evidence that a Curtiss YC-30 might have served as a presidential aircraft during the mid-1930s. (Curtiss Photo)

Douglas Dolphin RD-2

Many are unaware of the long-forgotten Dolphin RD-2, one of which was an early presidential plane, even though it never carried the president. It was the first of three RD-2s ordered. Under Navy control, and painted dark Navy Blue by the way, the plane was moored in the Potomac River with the crew having to stand in knee-deep water to perform maintenance.

As time went by, the presidential mission became a secondary mission, second to the hauling of mail and guests to FDR, especially when he was staying aboard the presidential yacht. The plane carried a removable presidential patch near the nose of the aircraft. Later, a second RD-2 would also be assigned to the president, but he would never fly in that one, either.

Boeing Dixie Clipper

Surprisingly enough, it was the commercial airline industry that provided the first transport in which the president first flew. The first presidential take-off actually occurred aboard one of the famous Pan American Clippers, coined at the time the "Dixie Clipper."

At the time the Navy had contracted for the use of several of these Clippers during the war. And so, on January 11, 1943, FDR took off in one of the planes from a seaplane base near Miami. The purpose of the trip was the historic meeting with Winston Churchill in Casablanca. For obvious safety reasons, the Clipper flew the overwater legs of the journey. The overland portions of the trip were made with four-engine C-54s flown by TWA crews.

This 1933 photo shows a particular Douglas Dolphin RD-2 which was designed to carry mail along with also transporting President Roosevelt. (Douglas Photo)

President Roosevelt with advisors and guests aboard the Boeing Clipper during 1943. The occasion was his 61st birthday. (USAF Photo)

There was no mistaking the Dixie Clipper, actually on loan from Pan American Airways, with the large block lettering on the nose. (USAF Photo)

The Dixie Clipper carried few of the luxury items that might be expected aboard a presidential aircraft. About the only special request that was granted was that one berth be equipped with a double mattress. Besides a few upholstered chairs and a camouflage paint scheme, the Clipper was little different from a standard version.

Lt. Howard Cone, a PanAm Captain on active duty, and his ten-man crew knew that they would be carrying an important person aboard the Dixie Clipper, but they certainly never imagined it would be President Roosevelt.

Lt. Cone was only told that he would be carrying nine passengers who were listed as number 1, number 2, etc. When passenger number 1 stepped into the Clipper's lounge, Lt. Cone nervously snapped a salute and found the right words, "Mr. President, I'm glad to have you aboard, sir." FDR quickly put him at ease by shaking his hand.

An identical Pan American Clipper, the "Atlantic Clipper," flew along as an escort and served as a communications center so that FDR could keep in touch with Washington and the war news from overseas.

FDR amazed the crew with his ability to navigate. On some maps the crew provided him, he was able to pick out the route he took on a pack trip to Haiti several years earlier.

Besides being the first flight by a president in office, the trip made other history. No other president had traveled to Africa, or even left the United States during wartime. And no president since Lincoln had visited a battlefield. The trip had another first that will be remembered by the crew when the president celebrated his 61st birthday aboard the plane.

The Dixie Clipper shown during a take-off in the early 1940s. (USAF Photo)

An early photo of the Dixie Clipper while it was still in Pam Am livery. Note the large American flag on the nose. (PanAm Photo)

The American flag had been removed in this shot of the Dixie Clipper, but the Pan Am lettering and emblem were still in place. The huge plane, an early wide-body, was actually a double-deck model which provided considerable volume. (Boeing Photo)

That first presidential flight was considered a tremendous success. In the trip to and from Casablanca, the two Clippers covered 11,000 miles without an incident. They were in the Clipper almost three full days, touched down on three continents, crossed the equator four times, and the Atlantic Ocean twice. Not until the Clippers reached their moorings in New York, after dropping off their very-important passenger in Miami, were all the personnel involved in operation told that they had helped fly the president.

Douglas C-54

As previously mentioned, FDR transferred from the flying boat to a C-54 for the overland portions of the journey. After the ten-day conference at Casablanca, FDR also made a two thousand mile side trip to Liberia using two C-54s piloted by TWA crews. Major Otis Bryan, then a TWA Vice President, had the honor of being the presidential pilot for this trip.

Captain Bryan recalled a rare occasion to meet one of the great leaders of the world. He fondly recalled a particular departure from Cairo. Just before takeoff, Winston Churchill came running down the runway to say goodbye to FDR.

Being still quite early in the morning, the usually conservatively-dressed British Prime Minister was wearing only his pajamas and a robe. FDR insisted that a photographer take a picture of this amusing scene, much to the chagrin of Sir Winston.

It was not all perfect for the plane. Once, on an approach, a hydraulic pump failure made flap lowering impossible. When told of the problem, FDR assured Bryan and the crew by telling them to do the best they could, and added, "We'll have a good time." Aside from a faster than usual landing, everything was normal.

3

Guess Where II C-87

The Presidential plane with the strange name—a modified C-87 military transport which would be unofficially coined the Guess Where II—could well have been the first aircraft built specifically to carry the President. To verify that statement, the plane was actually assigned to the White House during the 1943/44 time period.

The earlier flights of the President served to guide the configuration of the new model with two serious requirements. Long range came first, a capability that would enable the plane to make long overwater flights without having to make servicing stops, which created security worries.

And also, since the President during this period was Roosevelt, it was necessary to accomodate his wheel chair. Other aircraft, because of their fuselage height required 30-foot ramps to wheel FDR into the cabin. Such was not the case with the C-87, which sat very low to the ground. It was so low, in fact, that the President could be hand-carried into the cabin.

The C-87 also had a lot going for it in fulfilling the long range requirement. The model was actually a transport version of the Consolidated B-24 Liberator bomber, a craft that obviously had great range which it had demonstrated on round-trip bombing missions from England to the German heartland.

The C-87 was in mass production during the early 1940s at the Consolidated plant in Fort Worth, with the planes being built under Contract Number A.C. 18723. It is not known what the selection criteria was, but three planes were selected to serve this special mission requirement. An interesting note about this trio of planes was that the Consolidated workers were not informed of their special mission.

The planes were all assigned to Washington National Airport, with one of them, Number 159, being specifically assigned to the president. All of them, though, were a part of the famous "Brass Hat Squadron."

A little-known fact about that special plane of planes was that a C-54 fuel tank was added for even greater range. The tank was located directly below the cabin floor, and the fuel could be heard sloshing about until it was burned off.

It was not evident from the interiors of the planes which one was the real item since they were all identical. Taking a custom of the railroad industry, four Pullman-style compartments were placed on the right side of the fueslage. There were also a pair of lavatories and a complete aircraft galley.

On the left side of the cabin was a sofa-type seat and other furniture. It was so arranged that this compartment, along with a lavatory, could be isolated from the rest of the cabin by a curtain. The planes could sleep nine, or seat about 20 passengers. It was pretty plush stuff for the time period.

Of course, during wartime, it was a prime goal to keep the planes as inconspicuous as possible. Externally the transports, in their olive drab paint, looked no different from their C-87 brothers. The only identifier for the plane were the standard American insignia on the sides of the fuselage and the five yellow block numbers, 124159, on each of the twin tails.

The next presidential aircraft actually evolved from a bomber, namely the World War II legend, the B-24 Liberator. Along with the B-17 Flying Fortress, the plane was one of the reasons that World War II was won. (Army Air Force Photo)

With its cavernous fuselage, the B-24 made an excellent candidate to also be converted into a transport, a transformation that was accomplished often. It was called the C-87, and one of its number would become a presidential aircraft. (Pratt & Whitney Photo)

Note that the fuselage of this C-87 (not the presidential aircraft) sports seven square windows in its lower fuselage. Those windows were not present in the presidential version. (Consolidated-Vultee Photo)

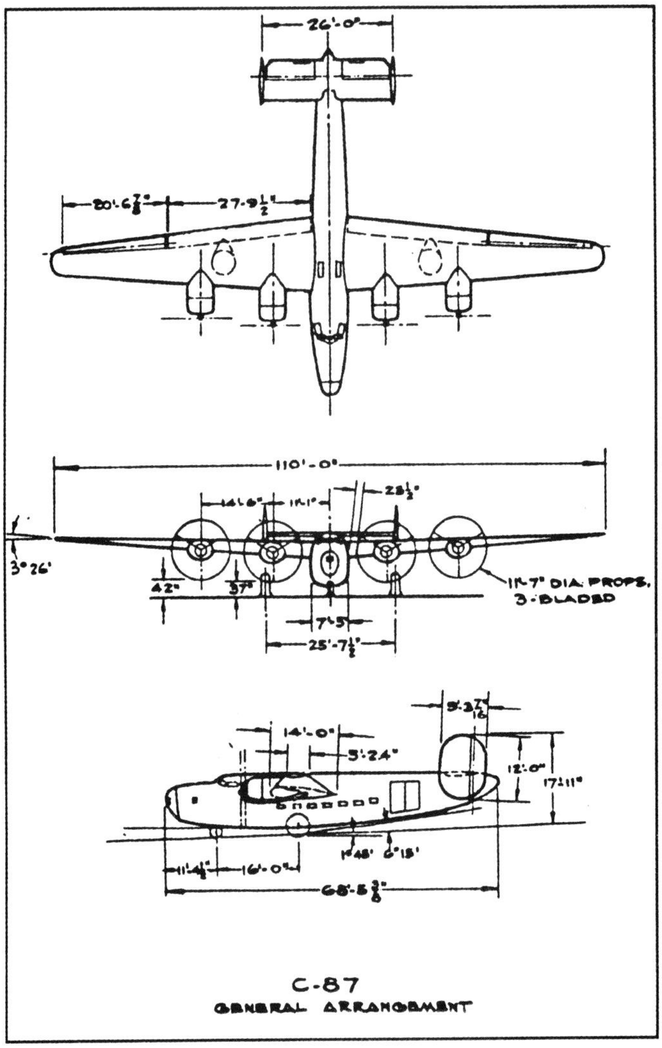

This drawing shows the dimensions of the C-87 Liberator express. Obviously, all the guns that were a part of the B-24 were removed. (Consolidated-Vultee Drawing)

However, to a sharp observer, the window spacing was different in these special planes. It goes without saying that it was a far cry from the blitzy detailing on the magnificent Air Force Ones of today.

The presidential pilot was selected with Major Henry Meyers, a former American Airline pilot, getting the prestigious assignment. He received special training before assuming his duties.

The plane was flown to Washington National Airport in June 1941, and shortly thereafter it received its interesting name, the Guess Where II. Rumor has it that it was named after a similarly-modified DC-3B (C-84), which was the Guess Where.

In line with the covert nature of its mission, there certainly was no celebration on the Guess Where II's arrival at National Airport. The only recognition of the plane's existence were the additional guards noted around the aircraft. The plane was then allowed to blend in with the other military aircraft in the same general area.

For the year that the plane held its esteemed position it made a number of international flights, including a well-recorded around-the-world flight in 1943 with a number of U.S. Senators and high-ranking military aboard.

The most famous flight, though, was made with the President's wife, Eleanor, on board for a 13,000 mile flight to the southern hemisphere. It was basically a flight to raise the morale of troops that were stationed there out of the combat zone to assure them that their job was important, too.

It would be the closest that the President would come to flying on his designated transportation. One flight had actually been scheduled for him for November 1943, but there was worry about a tail-buffet problem that was being experienced by B-24s and C-87s.

For that reason it was decided that the plane would not be used. It was later discovered that there was no serious

This photo shows the Guess Where II, along with Eleanor Roosevelt, crew, and passengers. About the only identification of the plane was the standard stars and bars fuselage insignia and the 124159 tail number. (USAF Photo)

problem to worry about with the phenomina, since it was caused when the cowl flaps of the engines were in the open position. Even though the model had many positives, it was decided that the plane could be surpassed by the Douglas C-54 model.

The plane stayed with the Special Air Missions Fleet. Following arrival of the C-54 Presidential Aircraft (i.e. the Sacred Cow), the plane spent time at other bases until the end of the war.

After it had been replaced, The Guess Where II actually went along as a back-up plane on a mission to Cairo in case its easy loading capabilities might be required. During one phase of this mission, the plane was actually fired upon by the British when identification was not recieved in time. Fortunately, the plane was not damaged.

On October 30, 1945, the Guess Where II made what was probably its final flight to Walnut Ridge, Arkansas, a location for the dismantling of military aircraft. Although it cannot be firmly ascertained, it is estimated that the plane met its demise being cut up for scrap.

In retrospect, it was a sad ending for the first official presidential aircraft. Since all the planes that followed the Guess Where II have been restored, it is a shame that this plane could not have joined them. But it was the end of the war, and things such as preserving an aircraft that was designed to fly the president were about as far from the minds of the victors as possible.

4
Sacred Cow C-54

Granted, the President had flown on other transports before the subject of this chapter, but the so-called "Sacred Cow" was the first official Presidential Aircraft.

As you might suspect, the Sacred Cow name was not the official name given to the new plane, but one supposedly given by Washington newsmen. The Air Force had attempted to have the plane officially known as "The Flying White House," but that name would never be adopted.

This program tagged a specific C-54 to become the presidential transportation. The program began in the fall of 1943 with the initiation of "Project 51" between the Army Air Force and the Douglas Aircraft Corporation.

Since extreme care and security were important in its construction, the particular plane (factory serial number 7470) was pulled from the production line and moved to a secluded part of the plant. There, during the assembly and outfitting of the special plane, workmen were watched closely by both civilian and military inspectors.

President Roosevelt's crippled condition was again a paramount consideration in designing the interior. Some rather elaborate modifications allowed FDR to move about the interior in his wheelchair, including even sitting in the cockpit. The interior decore was not plush by today's standards, but it was pretty luxurious by 1940s standards.

A view of the Sacred Cow being restored at the Air Force Museum. (Air Force Museum Photo)

Some of the more interesting furnishings included a stateroom with a conference table, upholstered swivel chairs, a large bullet-proof picture window, and two electrically-operated folding chairs. Even so, it was pretty cramped quarters for FDR and his staff of six.

It was quickly realized that special wheelchair ramps around an airport would be a dead give-away that FDR would be using that particular airfield. During wartime, this would be

This particular Douglas C-54 was selected for a very important mission, that being to serve as the next presidential aircraft. (Douglas Photo)

Ramp shots were always good photo ops. Here, President Truman and his wife emerge from the Sacred Cow. (USAF Photo)

a risky situation. Therefore, a special battery-operated elevator was installed which brought its passenger from the ground to cabin floor height in one easy motion. This innovative system did away with the tell-tail ramps.

So that the president could see outside, a large bullet-proof window was installed near the front of the plane. Interestingly enough, this was the only armor-plating portion of the craft, with the rest of the fuselage being totally vulnerable. The rest of the plane was made out of the standard thin aluminum, and was hardly any match for even a small caliber bullet.

"Looking like any other C-54" was one of the most important thoughts in the designers' minds. The elevator modification did not show, and a special template was constructed to place over the bullet-proof window to make it look like all its C-54 brothers.

Also, there were no fancy trappings on the outside of the plane, just normal military markings. It certainly was a far cry from the snazzy-painted presidential planes that would follow.

Offical circles tried to discourage the use of the Sacred Cow nickname, but with no luck. The name, obviously, was never painted on the bird, nor was it every officially accepted.

After all the work that had gone into the Scared Cow, FDR would only use it one time before his death in 1945.

This photo shows the flight crew of the Sacred Cow in a publicity shot. (USAF Photo)

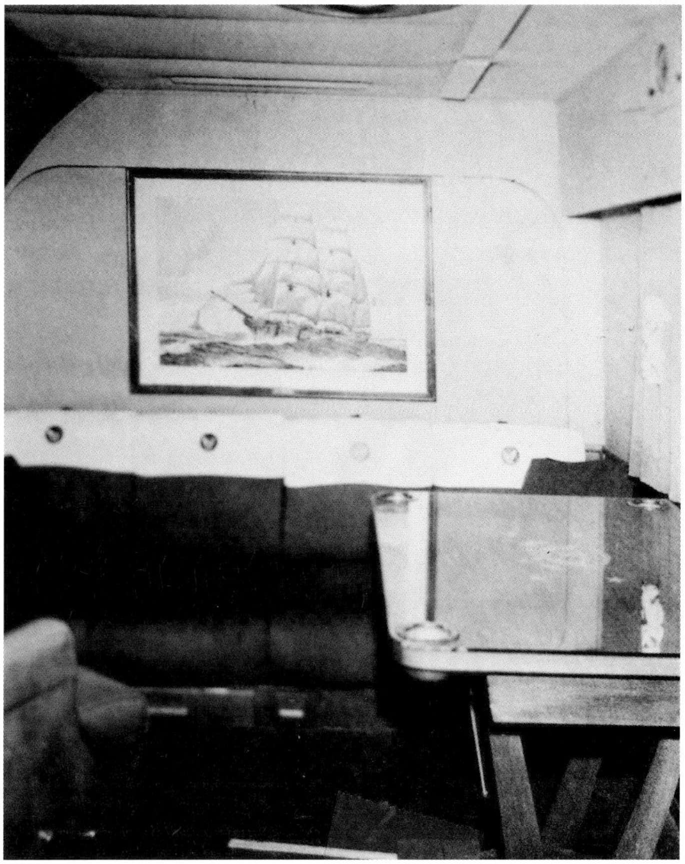

This is the cabin compartment within the Sacred Cow showing the seating accomodations. (USAF Photo)

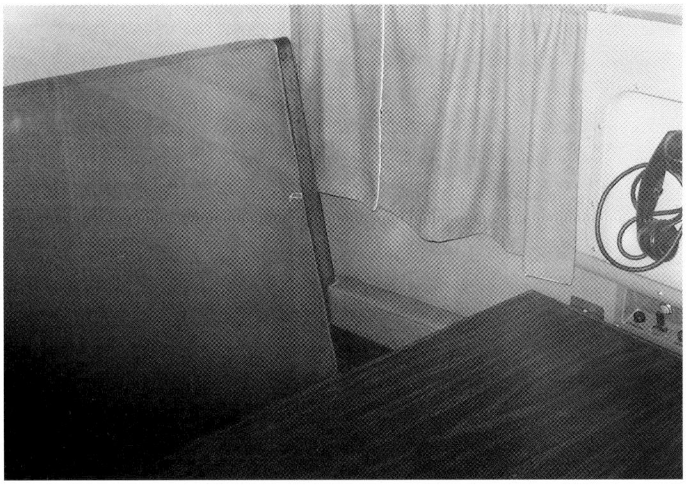

Plush for the period, the interior of the Sacred Cow appears a bit austure by today's standards. (Bill Holder Photo)

A view down the main aisle of the Sacred Cow. This is the restored Sacred Cow at the Air Force Museum, with clear plastic walls on either side protecting the historical contents. (Bill Holder Photo)

This voyage occurred on his trip from Malta to Yalta, a trip on which the famous passenger traveled under the codename "Sawbuck" for security reasons. It should be noted that Roosevelt was not particularly enchanted with air travel, having made only three flights while in office.

But the Sacred Cow's first official flight came earlier, on July 1, 1944, when it transported a group of government officials to Europe. It was necessary to stop at Casablanca, at which time it picked up a fighter escort as it made the final leg of its trip. Later, on at least one occasion, the plane's serial number was changed for safety reasons.

But FDR was not the only VIP to use the Cow during its flying days during the war. Winston Churchill, Mme. Chang Kai-Shek of China, along with U.S. Government officials all used the plane on occasion.

After FDR's death, the Cow remained unchanged for its new tenant-President Harry Truman, who made his first flight in the plane on May 5, 1945, the origin of the flight being Kansas City, Missouri.

Even the now-unnecessary elevator was retained. Somehow, it just did not seem right to remove it. When the war ended, it was decided to decorate the Cow for its many trips in carrying dignatories around the world. Forty-four flags were painted on the nose to signify the countries the plane had touched down in during its important missions. Just like fighters and bombers that sported their "kills," the Cow showed how it too had helped win the war.

A view of the sink and stove within the kitchen of the Sacred Cow. It has a bit of a modern look about it. (Bill Holder Photo)

Looking through the protective walls at the instrument panel inside the Sacred Cow. (Bill Holder Photo)

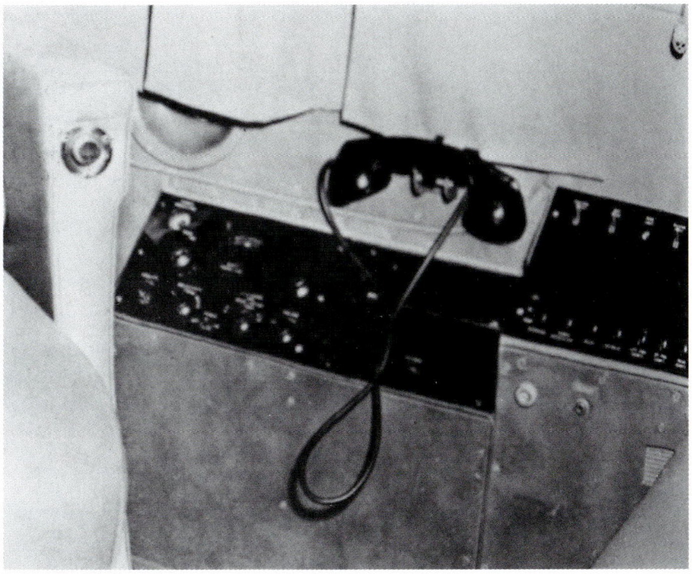

The communications center on the Sacred Cow, which provided limited capabilities. (USAF Photo)

A view of the co-pilot's location in the Sacred Cow on display at the Air Force Museum. (Bill Holder Photo)

On July 26, 1947, President Truman signed the National Security Act of 1947 while on board the Sacred Cow. This act established the U.S. Air Force as an independent service, making the plane the birthplace of the U.S. Air Force.

In 1947, the Sacred Cow bid goodbye to its White House duties, and for the first time, joined its C-54 contemporaries in the "real Air Force." During its Presidental tour, it had flown 1,900 hours and over 425,000 air miles.

The grand old lady was officially retired from the active Air Force in 1961 at an impressive ceremony in Washington. Then, she just sat and sat at the Smithsonian Institution, supposedly waiting to be restored back to her presidential configuration.

The restoration did not happen at that location. In 1983, it was transferred by truck to the Air Force Museum, where it would later be restored back to its original configuration in an awesome ten-year, 34,000 manhour effort.

The plane now appears on display at the museum as it did during President Roosevelt's trip to Yalta. The plane is open for touring and certainly brings back memories when it was the country's number one plane!

Looking back along the fuselage of the Sacred Cow, whose sheet metal has been brought up to a high luster. (Bill Holder Photo)

The Sacred Cow, even after its many years of service, still carries a majestic look. (Bill Holder Photo)

A view of the elevator that was used by President Roosevelt for use on the Sacred Cow. (Bill Holder Photo)

The Sacred Cow could be easily identified by this 252 numbering with the yellow background on the front of the nose. (Bill Holder Photo)

The wheel chocks on the Sacred Cow at the Air Force Museum carry the Sacred Cow nomenclature. (Bill Holder Photo)

Looking forward on the left side of the Sacred Cow. (Bill Holder Photo)

5
The Independence DC-6

The next presidential aircraft was also built by Douglas, since it was really a DC-6 (C-118 in military jargon), similar to those used by the airlines in the 1950s and 1960s.

The plane was quickly dubbed "The Independence" before she picked up an "undignified" name like the Sacred Cow. The presidential pilot, Lt Colonel Henry Myers, chose the name for two very good reasons. The plane was put into service on Independence Day of 1947, and President Truman's hometown was Independence, Missouri.

Myers remained the Independence's pilot until 1948 when he returned to American Airlines. He was replaced by Lt Col Francis Williams, who performed the duties for the remainder of the Truman term of office.

The Independence had all the latest aircraft innovations of the day, including reversable pitch propellers, water injection for extra power during take-off, and weather avoidance radar. With additional onboard fuel tanks, the model had a range of about 4,400 miles.

During its presidential tenure, there were also a number of updating modifications made to the plane. In 1948, a stabilizer antenna and new radome were added. Then, in 1952, a new APS-42 radar system was incorporated, which required yet another new radome system to accomodate the most advanced radar system.

A later paint scheme for The Independence featured more white on the nose of the plane. (McDonnell Douglas Photo)

The Independence introduced the snazziest paint job yet seen, surpassing all of the the presidential planes that preceeded it, and even some that followed it.

With its unique forward-fuselage paint scheme, there was no mistaking The Independence when it made an appearance. (McDonnell Douglas Photo)

A closer view of the later white nose of The Independence in its restored state at the Air Force Museum. (Bill Holder Photo)

The tail-feather-like tail design for The Independence is clear in this photo. Note the United Air Lines DC-6s that joined The Independence on the McDonnell Douglas flight line. (McDonnell Douglas Photo)

The theme of the blue-dominated paint scheme was an American Eagle with a light blue fuselage strip and tail feathers, navy blue head feathers, and a gray beak. This painting was then outlined with a yellow pin stripe.

A little-known fact is that the paint scheme was originally intended for American Airlines, but the airline discarded it when the interest of using it for the presidential plane was solidified. The Air Force did not come up with the $1500 to pay Douglas for the extra paint frill, but Douglas finally threw in the paint job free of charge.

Margaret Truman, daughter of the president, was the first member of the First Family to fly on the Independence. The plane would also later be used to return the body of the Greek Ambassador back to Greece shortly after it was commissioned in 1947.

One of the most famous flights of the plane occurred in October 1950 to Wake Island in the Pacific when President

The blue stripe on The Independence ran the length of the fuselage, terminating under the vertical stabillizer. (USAF Photo)

The Independence served as the background for many official government press conferences. (USAF Photo)

The livery of The Independence gave it a completely different look from its airline brethren. (USAF Photo)

The Independence was under the control of the Air Force's Air Transport Command as shown by this emblem on the sides of the fuselage. (Bill Holder Photo)

On display at the Air Force Museum, The Independence has been restored to exacting accuracy. (Bill Holder Photo)

An Air Force guard watches over The Independence on the ramp at Andrews Air Force Base, Maryland. (USAF Photo)

Truman met with General MacArthur to discuss the Korean War situation.

Externally, this C-118 appeared only slightly different from standard-production DC-6s. The most noticeable difference in this version were the three closely-grouped windows on the starboard side of the fuselage.

Internally, there was a presidential state room entered through a mahogany door bearing the presidential seal. Passenger-wise, the plane was capable of carrying only 25, as opposed to the normal load of 52 passengers. There was also the capability to sleep a dozen passengers.

The Independence remained the presidential aircraft until 1953, also serving President Eisenhower for a short time, before it was assigned to the Military Air Transport Service (MATS) and assigned Special Air Missions flights from Bolling Air Force Base.

During this period, it still carried distinguished passengers. Four months after the assignment, the plane lost its

The Independence at the Air Force Museum is open to the public which can wonder through the historical plane. (Bill Holder Photo)

Note the large window directly under The Independence lettering on the forward fuselage. (Bill Holder Photo)

The Independence still carries its prestige after all these years. (Bill Holder Photo)

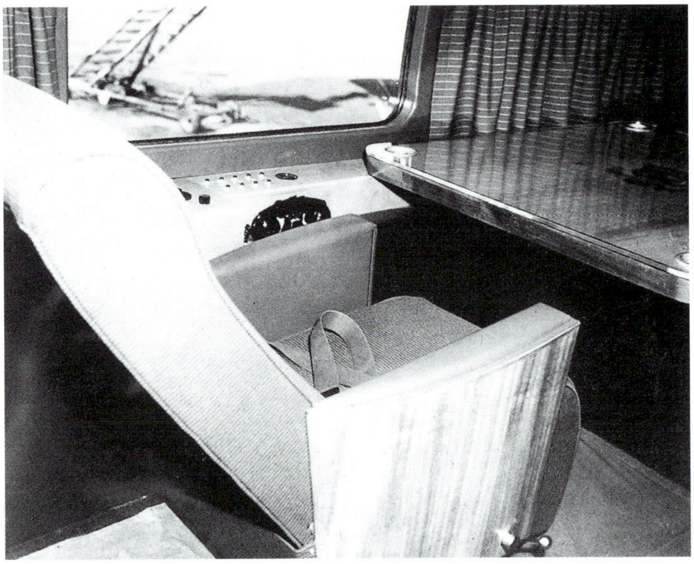

A view of the conference area of The Independence, while looking out one on the plane's large windows. (USAF Photo)

Even though The Independence was the nation's number one aircraft, its interior was still pretty austere, as can be seen by this photo taken during Independence's active days. (USAF Photo)

The plane also had a normal passenger seating area, much like a standard airliner. (USAF Photo)

Like the other presidential planes in the Air Force Museum, there is a transparent wall which protects the plane's contents, but still enables the visitors to see the complete interior. (Bill Holder Photo)

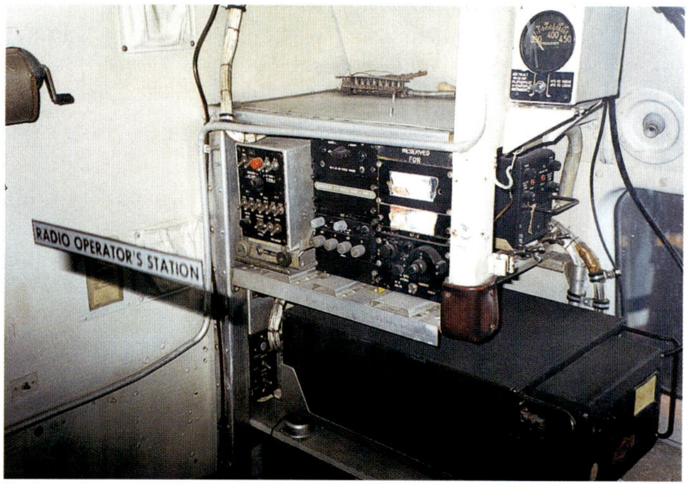

The Radio Operator's Station within The Independence. (Bill Holder Photo)

uniqueness when the presidential garb was removed and the plane went back to its normal USAF transport look.

But there was still a lot of missions left for this bird, and to accomplish them, new R-2800 engines were installed providing the plane with 1600 additional horsepower. The increased performance of the former Independence enabled it to set a coast-to-coast transport speed record.

Later, the plane continued to perform missions from Andrews Air Force Base before being assigned to McDill AFB, Florida, in 1963. In 1964, it joined the Tactical Air Command as a command support aircraft. After more than 18 years of faithful service, old number 46-505, as it was carried in official USAF records, was retired from the USAF fleet, and later transferred to the Air Force Museum in 1965.

Since it had lost its presidential livery, the plane was accurately restored back to that unique look by museum employees, and today, it is on display at the museum with a number of other presidential aircraft.

The Independence would later take on one other livery as part of the United States Strike Command organization. (USAF Photo)

The Independence after its retirement from presidential duties and return to the presidential fleet. (USAF Photo)

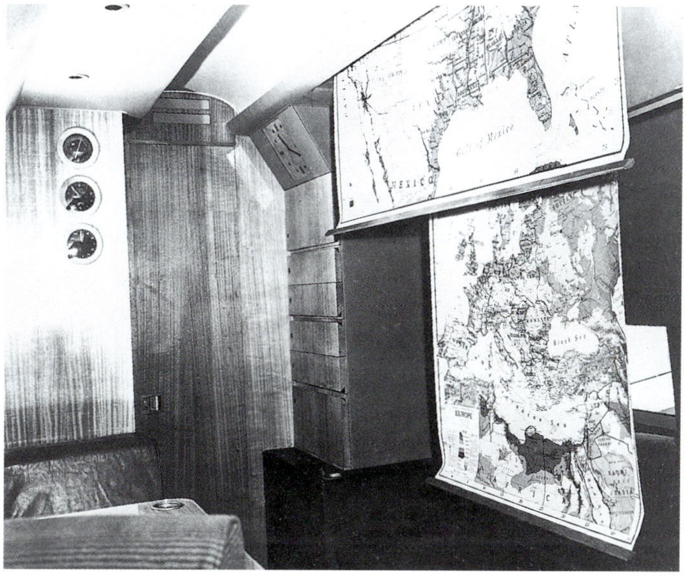

Maps and clocks adorn the walls of this conference room inside The Independence. (USAF Photo)

6

Columbines I and II C-121As

When General Eisenhower was assigned duties as Supreme Commander, Allied Powers Europe, the United States government placed at his disposal a Lockheed C-121A Constellation, the tail number originally being 8614, and later changed to 80614. The Constellation was selected as a replacement for the aging C-54s which had previously performed the VIP transportation function.

This was the first of three Columbines, being unofficially called Columbine I. Eisenhower's office at the time noted that the aircraft was in an international pool, and while flown by USAF personnel, it was not considered a U.S. plane.

Captain William Draper was selected as the pilot of this aircraft. Soon, the name Columbine—personally selected by General Eisenhower himself—was painted across the aircraft's nose in a flowing script. A representation of the Columbine flower, the official flower of Mamie Eisenhower's home state of Colorado, was painted underneath the name.

The plane remained in Europe after General Eisenhower returned to the United States. Later it would be assigned to USAFE Headquarters in Wiesbaden, Germany. When it was decommisioned, the plane was not saved because of its Eisenhower involvement. Although the first Columbine was not an official Presidential aircraft, it did transport a future President.

The Columbine I also must have played heavily in Ike's decision to select a similar model for his selection as the real item. Ike really liked the styling and flying characteristics of the Constellation, hence his selection of another C-121A Connie for the first official C-121A Presidential plane, Columbine II, and the second Columbine.

This particular C-121A, tail number 48-610, was selected by then-Major Draper because of its prior record of excellant performance, along with its already-existing VIP-style interior that was very applicable to its new Presidential mission requirement.

Prior to its Presidential duties, the plane had been stationed at MacArthur Field, New York. In that capacity, it flew many military missions before it was assigned to Washington, where it served top officials with the newly-created U.S. Air Force.

The Columbine II was the third official presidential aircraft and was done in bare metal with USAF markings. (USAF Photo)

A view of the Columbine II after it was returned to fleet service. Note that it has a completely new paint scheme. (USAF Photo)

After Eisenhower was elected and returned from his Korean flight, the plane was further altered and updated to his desires. The modifications were accomplished by the Burbank, California, Lockheed facility. Following the completion of the changes in February 1950, the plane was redesignated as a VC-121A.

During the course of its service the plane received numerous upgrades, including new engines, propellers, and landing gears to name a few. At the end of its career, the plane had signficantly greater performance and range.

Also, in late 1950, a weather radar was installed, to be followed later by a more advanced model. The incorporation of these systems resulted in a change of the shape of the plane's nose, giving it a longer, more graceful look, but necessary to accomodate the radar systems.

The interior was a step up from earlier presidential planes, being done in several grey tones. A large stateroom for conferences was in place in the plane's waist compartment. Contained were special chairs for both the president and his wife.

An advanced telephone system at the president's elbow enabled him to talk to the crew any time during flight. Another phone could be hooked into a land line for conversing while the plane was on the ground.

The mid-cabin also incorporated a pair of two long couches which were placed against the walls. The couches could be converted to beds for sleeping at night. Located on the walls were a number of state-of-the-art aircraft instruments for the president to observe should he desire. There was even a painting on the wall of the Columbine flower.

There were two additional cabins forward of the President's, capable of seating 16 and sleeping half that number. There was a large storage area located just forward of the tail section, with room for clothes and baggage, along with 30 parachutes.

The Columbine II would eventually be replaced by the III version, at which time it was returned to the SAM fleet where it served as a back-up to the new presidential plane.

Following completion of its active duty days, the plane was flown to Davis-Montham AFB for longtime storage. In the late 1980s, the plane was removed and restored back to its former presidential configuration. On April 5, 1990, it made its first flight and became a part of a flying museum.

7

Columbine III VC-121E

In 1954, the Lockheed Constellation parade continued with the third of the breed, the Columbine III, a 1049C Super Constellation. It was not a new plane, having over four thousand hours on it before taking on the presidential duties.

There was no mistaking the look of the third Columbine with the yellow scripted "Columbine III" directly below the cockpit on both sides of the fuselage. Directly below the name was the expected Columbine flower drawing, done in white and dark blue. Many feel that, even today, the Columbine III was the best-looking presidential plane ever! And that comparison even includes the modern sleek jet Air Force 1s.

Although externally this Constellation resembled the two Columbines that preceeded it, this was an entirely different bird, being over 18 feet longer and with a 730 gallon greater fuel capacity. That aspect allowed for much greater range capability of about 4,000 miles. The plane's square windows were different from the first two Columbines, as well.

Cruising speed was significantly increased over the Columbine II with the inclusion of more powerful Wright R-3350 turbo-compound engines. The four powerplants produced a total of 14,000 horsepower, definitely needed to push the 68 ton plane through the air.

The Columbine III was basically a Super Constellation, 115 feet in length, with a four thousand mile range, a maximum speed of about 370 miles per hour, with a cruise speed of 335 miles per hour.

The sleek transport also carried greatly-improved communications equipment, including an airborne teletype machine and an air-to-ground telephone system. This equipment allowed the president to maintain continuous contact with the White House from anywhere in the world. The plane received numerous upgrades during its presidential tour, including new propellers and landing gears.

The VC-121E was unique, being the only such model in Air Force service. The plane was actually selected from the Lockheed production line of the Navy version of the model, classified as the R7V-1. Its official designation was 53-7885.

Now-Lt. Col William Draper was the official pilot of Columbine III and piloted the delivery flight from Burbank, Cali-

The crew of the Columbine III is standing at attention in front of the magnificent plane. (USAF Photol)

The most famous of the Columbines was this Constellation, the Columbine III. (USAF Photo)

A view of the Columbine III when it was first put into service. The modified C-121 was numbered 57-685. (USAF Photo)

The Eisenhowers are shown emerging from the Columbine III after one of their many flights in the plane. (USAF Photo)

fornia, to Andrews Air Force Base on September 10, 1954. Mamie Eisenhower officially christened the plane on November 24th with a bottle of water flown in from Colorado. Shortly thereafter, the plane made its first official flight, carrying the president to Augusta, Georgia. Normally, the plane flew with a flight and ground crew of about 30 personnel.

A view of the famous nose of the Columbine III with its unique flower arrangement. (Bill Holder Photo)

A look at the sturdy undercarriage of the Columbine III as it is on permanent display at the Air Force Museum. (Bill Holder Photo)

The Columbine III was differentiated from the Columbine II by its square windows. (USAF Photo)

The presidential seal on the fuselage of the Columbine III. (Bill Holder Photo)

Looking down the long fuselage of the Columbine III at the Air Force Museum. (Bill Holder Photo)

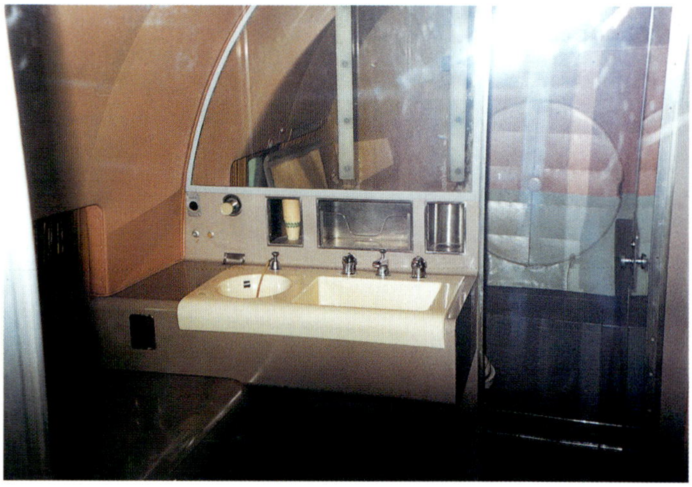

A sink within the Columbine III. (Bill Holder Photo)

The first overwater flight occurred in 1955, but the president was not aboard, the trip carrying the Secretary of State John Foster Dullas and other government officials.

The Columbine III was the longest-service presidential plane at the time, serving Eisenhower for some six years. And it certainly did not sit silently during the period, with frequent trips that averaged about 30,000 miles and over a hundred flying hours a year. Besides Ike's requirements, the plane was also used to carry foreign heads of state.

But even though the Columbine III had served well, the jet age was upon us at the time, and the grand old plane was decommissioned from its presidential duties on January 20, 1961.

The final Eisenhower flight aboard the aircraft was in December 1960, when he flew to one of his favorite vacation retreats, Augusta, GA, for a three-day visit.

Like the preceeding presidential planes, the Columbine III was assigned to the SAM fleet at Andrews AFB, where it joined two previous presidential birds.

Of course, the plane had its presidential markings removed and for a time was a completely silver aircraft. Then, it received the white solar resistant top and orange visibility markings.

On April 20, 1966, the great old bird made its final flight, this time to Wright Patterson AFB, where it was restored to its presidential configuration and installed in the Air Force Museum. There were a lot of old presidential friends there with which to socialize.

A historical note must be made about one other Constellation that almost became a presidential aircraft, but didn't quite make the call.

It was just before the 1948 presidential election when Governor Thomas Dewey was expected to easily defeat President Truman. Such was the assurance that this would happen that a Constellation, Air Force serial number 48-608, was planned to be Dewey's presidential bird. In fact, the plane had already been unofficially named the "Dewdrop" for its expected new resident.

A manniquin of President Eisenhower holds forth in the Columbine III. (Bill Holder Photo)

Other Columbine III accomdations. (Bill Holder Photo)

President Truman was not interested in adopting the C-121, being quite happy with The Independence he was currently occupying. The Dewdrop did, however, serve as a backup presidential aircraft, and also as an aircraft for the Secretary of the Air Force.

The Dewdrop, though, did have one unique distinction, setting a speed record from Washington to Burtonwood, England, in only 12 hours and eight minutes. The feat took place during the Christmas holiday of 1948, the same time that the Berlin Air Lift was being carried out.

The propeller tips of the Columbine III were painted in the traditional red, white, and blue. (Bill Holder Photo)

8

Tail Number 3240 C-118A

There was no fanfair and no construction of the next presidential aircraft. The plane already existed and was identified by its 3240 tail number.

With a change in the government administration in 1961, President Kennedy selected this model aircraft in the VIP fleet and designated it as the Presidential Aircraft. Nothing special about the aircraft, just a Douglas C-118A that had been delivered to the Air Force in December 1955.

With 3240, its C-118 designation might be confusing to some, but the plane was basically a DC-6A. When it was selected for presidential duties in 1961, it was certainly not new at seven years old, having been accepted by the Air Force six years earlier.

During its initial tenure, 3240 was assigned to the 1298th Air Transport (Special Missions) Squadron of the Military Air Transport Service (MATS), where it remained until its presidential duties in July 1961. It served as the presidential plane until January 1966.

With Robert Kennedy in a 1964 appearance, LBJ moves toward a waiting crowd with 3240(with 33240 designation on the tail). (Cecil Stoughton, LBJ Library-via Pima Air and Space Museum)

The 3240 Presidential Plane on display at the Pima Air and Space Museum. (Pima Air and Space Museum Photo)

President Johnson emerges from 3240 on October 15, 1964. (Cecil Stoughton, LBJ Library-via Pima Air and Space Museum)

A large business chair was available for presidential use in this faded period photo. (Air Force Museum Photo)

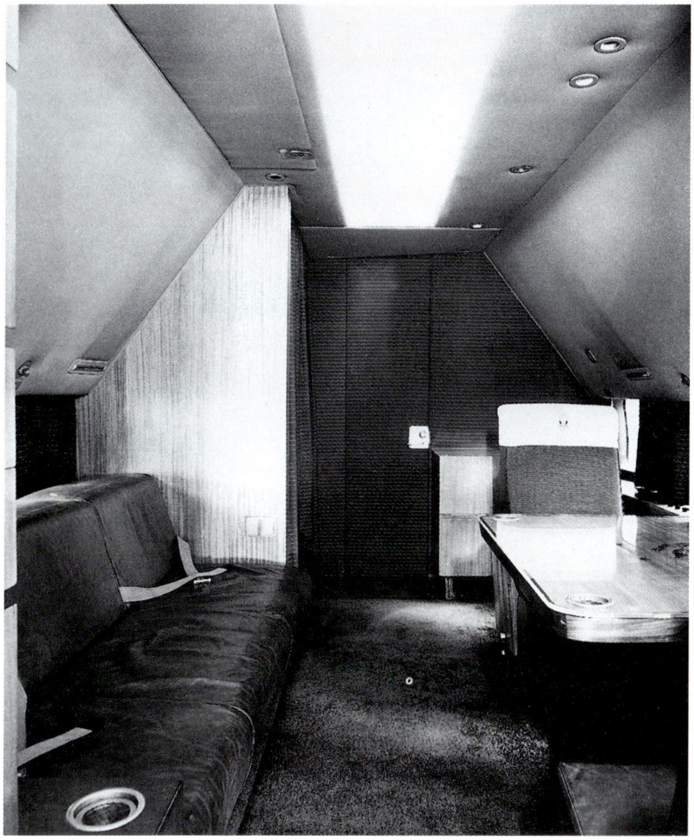

A view inside the 3240 craft still shows an interior far short of luxurious. The interior could best be described as more functional than fancy. (USAF Photo)

The Presidential Seal adorns the wall of one of the 3240 compartments. (Air Force Museum Photo)

Standard airliner seats were the standard in another portion of the plane. (Air Force Museum Photo)

An apparent short-wave radio was available in this desk aboard the 3240 plane. (Air Force Museum Photo)

The cockpit of this unique C-118A varied little from a standard C-118. (Air Force Museum Photo)

The 3240 after it was returned to the presidential fleet minus its presidential paint scheme. (Air Force Museum Photo)

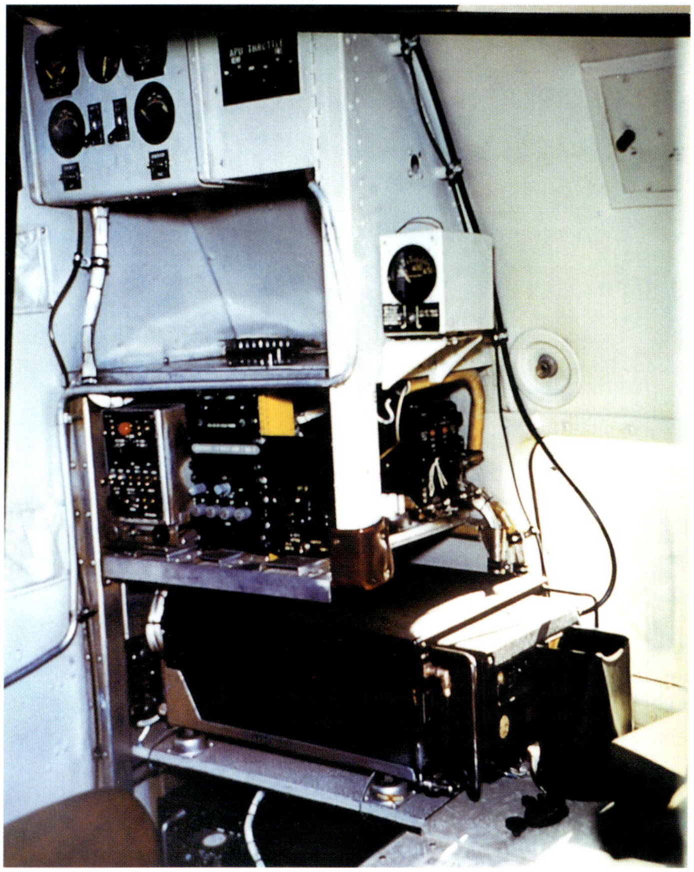

The kitchen aboard 3240 was done in stainless steel. (Air Force Museum Photo)

The 3240 radio operator's station. (Air Force Museum Photo)

It was during this time period that it also performed the VIP hauling duty. It transported many dignataries, but its main job had been to transport the Secretary of Defense.

An interesting coincidence occurred during 1961 when this C-118 replaced another of its presidential brethren, number 42-107451, which had affectionately been known as the Sacred Cow.

When 3240 was relieved of its presidential duties, it was assigned back to the USAF fleet and spent time at Chieves AB, France, Wiesbaden AB, Germany, and Randolph AFB, Texas. Then it was placed in storage in 1975 at Davis Montham AFB, Arizona, before being officially dropped from the USAF inventory as surplus in December 1976.

During its presidential days, 3240 ended up looking a lot like the current Air Force Ones, with the light blue and white paint scheme, along with the "United States of America" lettering stenciled down the length of the fuselage.

The plane was equipped with state-of-the-art equipment, with a high-frequency radio which enabled the president to communicate with the White House while in flight or on the ground in any part of the world. In addition, there was also an advanced-for-the-time duplex radio teletype system.

Otherwise, its appointments were pretty much the same as the other C-118 craft that were part of the VIP fleet. Outside, the presidential seal on the forward part of the fuselage was the only identifier to differentiate it from its fleet brothers. The 3240 was not configured for long-range flights and was used mostly for short hops. It is on display at the Pima Air & Space Museum in Tuscon, Arizona.

9

Tail Numbers 26000/27000 VC-137s

Without a doubt, it was the most famous of the presidential aircraft, and was the first to recieve widespread use of the "Air Force One" call sign.

Besides its long tenure, the two events that solidified its fame occurred on November 22, 1963, when the plane saw a new president (Lyndon B. Johnson) sworn in within its confines, along with carrying slain president (John F. Kennedy) back to Washington from Dallas, Texas.

Another historical first for the modified Boeing 707-300 took place as a result of its flying capabilities. In December 1967, the plane negotiated an around-the-world flight on official government business. The trip of over 28,000 miles took five days, including 59 hours and 30 minutes of flying time.

A later resident of the plane, President Nixon, flew the plane to the mid-Pacific in July 1969 for a rendezvous with the Apollo astronauts upon their return from the first moon landing. Nixon then continued on a 13-day around-the-world mission, covering more than 25,000 statute miles. The total flight time was over 53 hours and 40 minutes.

VC-137C, tail number 26000, initially arrived at Andrews Air Force Base on October 12, 1962, to join the MAC Special Missions Wing. In May 1963, the new Air Force One really showed what it could do with a record run between Washington and Moscow in eight hours 39 minutes. It broke 14 existing Air Force transport records.

President Nixon and family emerge from 26000. The stairs for the plane were carried on the back of a truck that was moved into position when boarding or deboarding was accomplished. (USAF Photo)

Guess it goes without saying that the capabilities of this magnificent bird far exceeded those of the previous presidential aircraft. With an altitude capability of over 43,000 feet, a cruising speed of 575 miles per hour, and an impressive range of 4,600 nautical miles, it is easy to see how much it

The most famous numbers to ever be carried on a presidential aircraft. (Bill Holder Photo)

The paint scheme of the 26000 presidential plane not only gave it a sleek look, but also a prestigious appearance. (USAF Photo)

The 26000 Air Force One VC-137 served many presidents in its long tenure. (USAF Photo)

exceeded the capabilities of previous presidential transports. It carried a crew of 23.

Needless to say, the interior of the plane was a lot different from its Boeing 707 brethren, being divided into a number of separate areas.

Just behind the cockpit was the communications center, which enabled the president to speak to any part of the world. Moving further back was the galley where the food was prepared. Next came the president's stateroom, which contained a bed, a lavatory, several chairs, and a phone. It was the location where the president could relax or work in private. Next in the walk to the rear of the plane came a conference room for holding meetings. Areas for the press corps and Air Force guards were provided in the far aft of the fuselage.

Each official occupant made some minor change for personal reasons, but it was President Kennedy who did the most

President Kennedy is shown deplaning from the rear of 26000 in this early 1970s photo. (USAF Photo)

President Johnson and his staff have a meeting at 40,000 feet aboard the 26000 Air Force One. (USAF Photo)

A souvenir of 26000 was this pair of match books which display a picture of the plane on one side and the Presidential Seal on the other side. (Bill Holder Photo)

modification. First, he wanted the exterior of the plane to be a proud advertisement of America.

To that end, he initiated the now-familiar "United States of America" blue lettering on the sides of the predominantly-white aircraft. The presidential seal was carried near the nose, and an American flag was located on the vertical tail. Before that, it was a military-appearing motif, being done in dayglow orange and white.

It is interesting to hear the stories of how the different presidents used the stately plane. President Johnson on more than one occasion hauled a load of White House residents down to his Houston home for a weekend at his Texas ranch. With Nixon and Kennedy, the atmosphere was more of dignity and decorum.

Reportedly, President Eisenhower had a restrained view of the new plane which he used during the final year of his second term. He had never flown on anything but prop-pow-

26000 carried airline windows just like the airliner version of the model. (Bill Holder Photo)

The 26000 still carries its grace and style while on display at the Air Force Museum. (Bill Holder Photo)

Looking at the wing root and fuselage of 26000 at the Air Force Museum. (Bill Holder Photo)

The communications center on 26000 enabled the president to maintain contact with the world situation while in flight. (Bill Holder Photo)

The furnishings aboard 26000 were a giant step upward from previous presidential aircraft. (Bill Holder Photo)

ered planes, and had a great love for the Columbine III. But the world was changing, and the need for a faster plane made 26000 a necessity.

From the number of tenants of any presidential planes, 26000 far exceeded all the others. There were an amazing eight presidents that flew on the plane, including Eisenhower, Kennedy, Johnson, Nixon, Ford, Carter, Bush, and Clinton.

It had a charisma all its own, loved by all that viewed it. It was the United States of America!

Since 26000 began flying in the electronic era, defending the plane against possible threats recieved a high priority. Surface to air missiles of increasing accuracy had been addressed, and this Air Force One was reported to have carried flairs to divert heat-seeking missiles. The plane also was estimated to have sophisticated jamming equipment to thwart radar-guided air-to-air missiles.

During the later years for the Boeing 707 presidential aircraft, the 26000 plane—which had accumulated considerable flight hours—was replaced by its twin 27000 backup plane.

Externally, the plane was practically identical to the original. 27000 etched its place in history in 1981 when it flew former Presidents Nixon, Ford, and Carter to Cairo, Egypt, to represent the United States at the funeral of Egyptian President Anwar Sadat. And, of course, it returned the body of President Kennedy from Dallas, TX, to Washington in 1963, certainly its saddest duty.

But, with its many historical flights, 26000 will obviously be the most-recalled of the planes. Also, 26000 has been retained in its presidential trim at the Air Force Museum. Standing proud, old 26000 looks like it could still perform the official missions that it did so well for so long.

Identical to 26000, the back-up 27000 VC-137 replaced the original as the primary Air Force One in the early 1980s. (USAF Photo)

10

Tail Number 28000 VC-25A

By the early 1980s, it was evident that there was a need for a replacement presidential aircraft to replace the long-reliable, but aging, 26000 and 27000 VC-137s. The search began in 1985 under the responsibility of the Air Force's Aeronautical Systems Division at Wright Patterson Air Force Base. The program was known as the Air Force One Replacement Program.

The Air Force stated that there were three significant reasons for the replacement. First, was the difficulty in maintaining and supporting the aging aircraft. The combined age of the existing Air Force One and its back-up was a combined service of 36 years. One plane had been purchased in 1962, and the other ten years later.

The Boeing 707, upon which the existing presidential plane was based, was being phased out of commercial airline service, which would greatly reduce the availability of spare parts worldwide. The acquisition of a new Air Force One definitely made good sense.

The second reason concerned the fact that 26000 and 27000 had no growth capacity. That is, the model could not accommodate newer and more complex communications equipment. Third, the VC-137 did not meet FAA standards and was limited in performance and range. With a longer-

During its flight test program, the new presidential birds didn't carry their presidential colors. (Boeing Photo)

One of the 747-based Air Force Ones is shown under construction at the Seattle Boeing facility. (Boeing Photo)

A close-up view of one of two very unique 747s under construction. (Boeing Photo)

A magestic sight, the VC-25A in flight replacing the longstanding VC-137 in the early 1990s. (Boeing Photo)

A brand-new VC-25A makes one of its first flights in 1990. (USAF Photo)

range plane, trips to far-away destinations could be made non-stop, greatly reducing security requirements by not having to refuel in foreign countries.

Specific performance and range requirements for the new design were specified with a minimum cruising speed of 538 miles per hour (Mach 0.8) required while flying at an altitude of between 36,000 and 45,000 feet. The cruise capability was required to be 575 miles per hour (Mach 0.88).

It was also specified that the new plane must be capable of providing seating for 80 passengers and 23 crew members, along with elaborate accommodations for the president and his staff. There were also to be galleys capable of preparing and serving some 50 meals from each galley.

An additional requirement was that the new presidential aircraft should be, if possible, a modification of an existing commercial aircraft. It came down to three candidates for the prestigious job, the Douglas DC-10 and two versions of the Boeing 747.

In 1986, it was decided that the -200B version of the 747 would serve as the basis for the new plane, basically an off-the-shelf version of the commercial 747 that had already been certified by the FAA. It was specified at the time that the new plane would be fitted with General Electric CF6-80C2B1 turbofan engines. Initially, it was planned that two of the planes would be procured, a prime and a backup.

The colors of the latest Air Force One blend beautifully with the ocean below. (USAF Photo)

The planes, which would carry the VC-25A designation, were built at Boeing's Seattle production plant using the normal assembly line process. Then, once the basic structures were completed, the planes were moved to Wichita, Kansas, for installation of the unique electronic and communications equipment and interior modifications. The first flight was scheduled for the summer of 1988, but it would be set back by production delays.

The planes were finally delivered in 1990, but their extravagance was not met with the exultation that was expected. President Bush was not happy about the cost of the planes when he indicated he was having to skimp on certain programs he was pushing to fund. Also, there was the fact that the cost of the planes had spiraled to $650 million, considerably higher that the initial contract amount of $265 million.

There were some objectors to the gigantic expenditure that suggested that possibly a pair of Boeing 767 airliners, at $25 million cheaper than a 747, could have been procured and modestly modified in order to accomplish the same mission. That, of course, did not happen, and undoubtedly these planes will be around for numerous decades of the 21st century.

The accommodations of these monsters are astounding. There are 85 telephones, a six-channel stereo, a six cubic foot safe for storing classified documents, and a television system that can pipe in eight channels simultaneously. The president also has the capability to view waiting crowds before emerging from the plane.

Additionally, there are four onboard computers, multiple copying machines, conference rooms, sleeper chairs, a complete press room, crew bunks, and many secure phone lines.

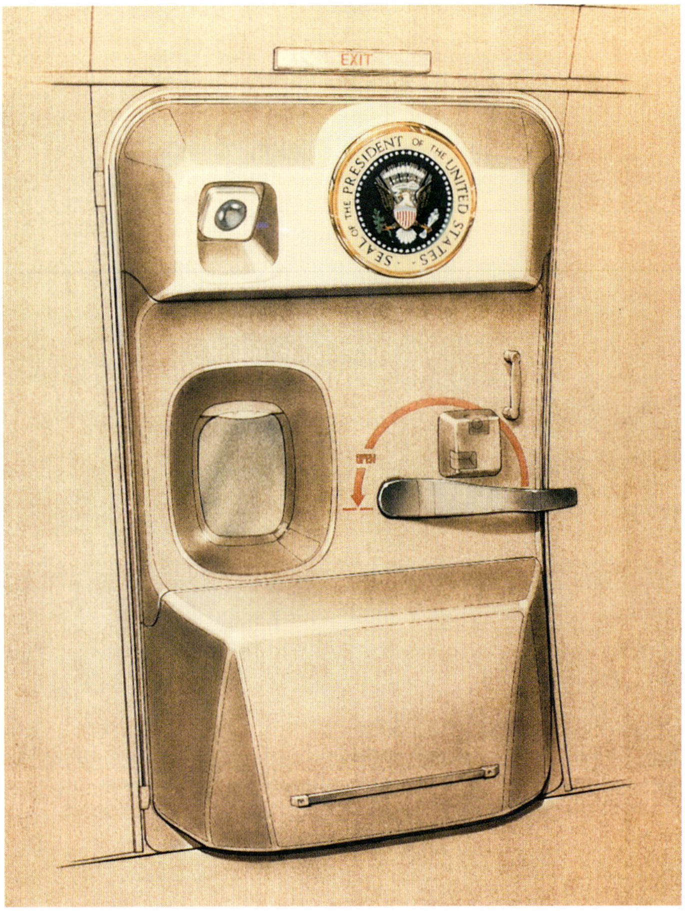

The Presidential Seal is prominantly mounted on the main entry door of the VC-25As as shown in this drawing. (USAF Drawing)

The same decorating style is continued throughout the plane. (USAF Photo)

There are something like six dozen antennas for the maze of electronic gear, with almost 250 miles of wire in place. That's more than twice the wire length for a standard 747 commercial version.

Since this is the president on board, a number of modifications were also made to deal with just about any contingency or emergency. For example, in the ceiling above the president's bedroom are two intravenous hookups.

Included in the plane's design was the capability for the president to exit the plane from an exit door in the lower rear fuselage should he not desire to negotiate the 26 feet of steps at the main exit door at the front of the plane.

The planes have even been hardened against an electromagnetic pulse from a nuclear explosion. It would seem that nothing has been forgotten, but without a doubt, through its future years of use, there will be additional changes made.

It has been reported that many of the changes that were made during the construction phase were responsible for the program's huge cost.

It had been hoped that the first plane could have been ready for President Reagen to fly before his term ended, since the plane had been conceived during his tenure. Unfortunately, though, that did not come to pass.

What did come to pass, though, is the awesome presence of these Air Force Ones, the biggest and by far the best ever, even if they did break the bank for their construction.

"Luxurious" would have to be the description of the Presidential Office within the VC-25A presidential aircraft. (USAF Photo)

Conference room aboard the 2800 Air Force One. Those chairs certainly look comfortable, don't they? (USAF Photo)

11

Presidential Support Planes

The beautifully-detailed Air Force One aircraft of today are probably the most recognized planes in the United States.

But when you think about it, you certainly can't fire up that big bird every time the president has to make a trip. It just isn't a practical situation, since many of the trips to be taken are a short trip across town, transportation from Air Force One itself at Andrews Air Force Base back to the White House, or a trip of several hundred miles.

Then, too, there are many other government and military officials that need quick transportation service, and smaller planes and helicopters fulfill these missions.

The Air Force, with its 89th Airlift Wing at Andrews Air Force Base, controls all the fixed wing presidential/VIP support aircraft (including Air Force One). The Marine Corps is in charge of all presidential/VIP helicopters from HMX-1 Marine Helicopter Squadron at Annicostia Naval Station. Following is a discussion of the planes of these interesting fleets, both past and present:

L-26(U-4B) Aero Commander

It really all began in the 1950s when there were a number of L-26 Aero Commanders located in the Washington, DC, area to carry around high-ranking Pentagon military officials. Then, in 1955, the Air Force ordered 15 L-26B versions of the small transport, but did not disclose at the time that the president planned to use one of them for his short-trip transportation.

President Eisenhower was anxious to have one of the new planes immediately, so a sales demonstrator was loaned to the Air Force by the manufacturer, a model 560 that was delivered in May, 1955. Upon delivery, the plane was quickly given its government livery with a Baltic Blue and Polar white

This L-26 Aero Commander was one of a number of the model that served with VIP transportation. This particular L-26 once carried President Eisenhower back and forth to his Gettyburg, PA farm. (USAF Photo)

This particular L-26 (also known as the U-4B) is on display at the Air Force Museum. (Bill Holder Photo)

paint job, the first presidential plane to receive the now-recognized Air Force One colors. Eventually, all of the 15 Aero Commanders that would serve would be painted in that same motif.

A month later, the plane made its first flight with Ike aboard to the president's farm in Gettysburg, PA. The flight lasted 32 minutes for the 73 air mile distance. Guess it goes without saying that a number of other small aircraft shadowed the plane to and from its destination.

In 1958, the Aero Commanders were given the new designation U-4B and continued to serve. U-4B 55-4647 remained in the service of the president until he retired from office in January 1960.

The plane still remained in government service until 1969, where it was used for transporting high-ranking government officials. Then, in October of that year, it was transferred to the Air Force Academy, where it was used for cadet parachute training and the Academy's skydiving team. In November 1977, the U-4B was sent to the Nebraska Civil Air Patrol. It was obtained by the Air Force Museum in 1996, restored to its presidential configuration, and then placed on permanent display.

A head-on view of the museum's U-4B. (Bill Holder Photo)

This is one of 11 Lockheed Jet Stars that was in the presidential support business. With 26 years of service, this plane has been on display at the Air Force Museum since 1987. (Bill Holder Photo)

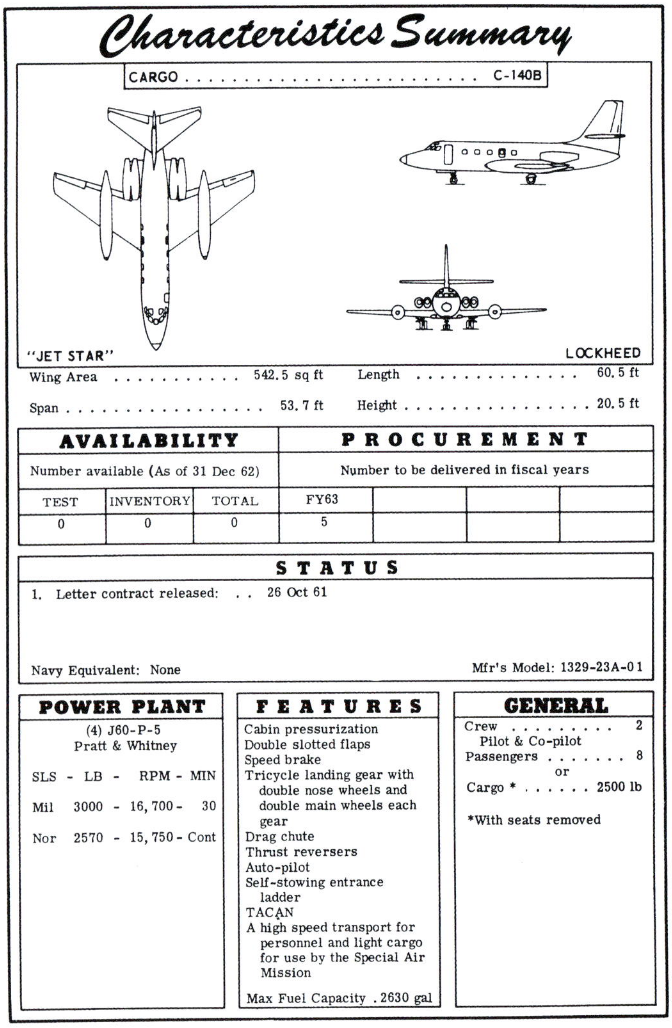

Characteristics Summary

CARGO C-140B

"JET STAR" LOCKHEED

Wing Area . . . . 542.5 sq ft — Length . . . . 60.5 ft

Span . . . . 53.7 ft — Height . . . . 20.5 ft

AVAILABILITY			PROCUREMENT			
Number available (As of 31 Dec 62)			Number to be delivered in fiscal years			
TEST	INVENTORY	TOTAL	FY63			
0	0	0	5			

STATUS

1. Letter contract released: . . 26 Oct 61

Navy Equivalent: None — Mfr's Model: 1329-23A-01

POWER PLANT

(4) J60-P-5
Pratt & Whitney

SLS	LB	RPM	MIN
Mil	3000	16,700	30
Nor	2570	15,750	Cont

FEATURES

Cabin pressurization
Double slotted flaps
Speed brake
Tricycle landing gear with double nose wheels and double main wheels each gear
Drag chute
Thrust reversers
Auto-pilot
Self-stowing entrance ladder
TACAN
A high speed transport for personnel and light cargo for use by the Special Air Mission

Max Fuel Capacity . 2630 gal

GENERAL

Crew 2
Pilot & Co-pilot
Passengers 8
or
Cargo * . . . . . . 2500 lb

*With seats removed

The military characteristics of the C-140 transport. (USAF Chart)

Lockheed VC-140B Jet Star

Eleven Lockheed Jet Star transports has served with the presidential fleet into the 1990s, where they flew a high percentage of the 89th missions. Due to range limitations, most of the missions were restricted to North and South America. All but two of the planes were painted in the distinctive Air Force One livery, with the other pair being completely white in color. Also, one of the VC-140s was assigned for vice presidential use. When the president was aboard one of these planes, it did carry the Air Force One designation when in flight.

The Jet Stars were highly instrumented, being equipped with Collins DN-101 doppler navigation systems, 618T-3 single sideband transceivers, and FD-105 and VOR-101 systems. There was VIP seating for six people, with power provided by four rear-mounted P&W 3,000 pound thrust J-60 turbojets.

One of those VC-140s is on display at the Air Force Museum, this particular model having served Presidents Nixon, Ford, Carter, and Reagen. This Jet Star served for 26 years and became a part of the Air Force Museum fleet in 1987.

Beechcraft VC-6A King Air

This aircraft type was placed in operational service in early 1966. During the early part of its career, it was used to transport President Lyndon Johnson and members of his family between Bergstrom AFB, Texas, near Austin, and the Johnson family ranch near Johnson City.

While serving the president, the aircraft informally became known as the "Lady Bird Special." After leaving presidential service, this VC-6A continued in its special executive transport mode with the 89th Airlift Wing until it was retired to the Air Force Museum in 1985.

In its U.S. Government trim, this VC-140 sits on the ramp at Andrews Air Force Base, Maryland. (USAF Photo)

The Air Force Museum also has a Beechcraft VC-6A King Air that performed presidential duties. (Bill Holder Photo)

Convair VC-131H

Even with the presidential fleet becoming almost completely jet powered, there were also some prop-powered transports as late as the 1970s. General Dynamics/Convair VC-131Hs were used by the 89th for high priority domestic travel until they were replaced in the mid-1970s. Plans to upgrade the planes earlier with an improved weather radar were canceled because of the imminent replacement of the model. The VC-131s were returned to the USAF inventory upon completion of their VIP tours.

Boeing VC-137

In 1958, under the project name "Out Front," a number of VC-137s were intoduced to the presidential fleet. The planes were periodically modified by Boeing during their long tenures, along with being retrofitted with more-powerful JT3D turbofan engines.

The planes were the workhorses of the 89th through the years. Another VC-137, 26000, was of course the actual Air Force One. Another of those models, tail number 27000, served as a back-up to 26000 in performing presidential duties.

McDonnell-Douglas DC-9 Nightingale

Designed initially as a medical evacuation transport for its military duties, there were also a number of DC-9s that played in the presidential support mission. Stationed at the 89th Airlift Wing, the DC-9s were painted in the normal blue and white color scheme.

Gulfstream Aerospace VC-20 Gulfstream

The VC-20 Gulfstream entered the presidential fleet following the VC-140. In addition to its presidential duties, the VC-20 has proved to be a flexible small transport, fulfilling a number of official missions.

Helicopter Support Aircraft

In 1957, HMX-1 was given the additional responsibility of providing short-range transportation for the president and government VIPs. The duty was quickly undertaken, with Presi-

A view of the museum's VC-140 looking back along its sleek fuselage to the pair of rear-mounted engines. (Bill Holder Photo)

The Presidential Seal is located on the forward fuselage of this VC-140. (Bill Holder Photo)

Note that the VC-6A carries a blue and white paint scheme that is similar to the presidential paint scheme. (Bill Holder Photo)

One of the early VC-137s that was a part of the presidential fleet. The bright orange paint on the cockpit and tail were for visibility reasons. (USAF Photo)

dent Eisenhower making the first trip on September 7 of that same year from his summer home in Newport, RI, to a waiting Air Force One. The use of helicopters in this mission proved extremely efficient, greatly cutting the time the trip originally required.

The flight was accomplished in a UH-34 Seahorse helicopter. The success of this first mission prompted the White House to consider the possibility of landing an HMX-1 helicopter on the south lawn. The proposal was quickly evaluated as being totally feasible and was quickly implemented.

The most common trips that are carried out from this location were, and are, trips to and from Andrews Air Force Base and transfer to Air Force One. In 1976, the Marine Corps was assigned the responsibility of all helicopter transportation of the president and government officials within the United States.

The presidential duties of HMX-1 are performed by the Executive Flight Detachment, which employs the Skiorsky VH-3D Sky King and VH-60N Blackhawk. Because of their distinctive two-tone paint schemes with a white upper suface, the choppers have been coined the "White Tops."

The VH-3D is the prime presidential aircraft and is capable of carrying up to 14 passengers. The VH-60D carries three fewer passengers and is used for various White House missions. Both carry a crew of two, while the VH-60D also carries a communications systems operator.

Smaller in size than the VH-3D, the VH-60D can be folded up easily for transportation aboard a C-5A Galaxy transport for overseas assignments on short notice. The VH-60D can be prepared for loading on the C-5A in less than two hours!

The VH-60D has been in presidential service since the late 1970s, while the VH-3Ds have been around for about half that time.

Maintenance being performed on one of the VC-137s by 89th Airlift Wing personnel. (USAF Photo)

The DC-9 cuts a pretty picture in presidential garb. The model is a member of the presidential fleet and flies support missions. (USAF Photo)

Similar in appearance to the VC-140, the VC-20 followed but only had two rear mounted engines as compared to the four of the VC-140. (USAF Photo)

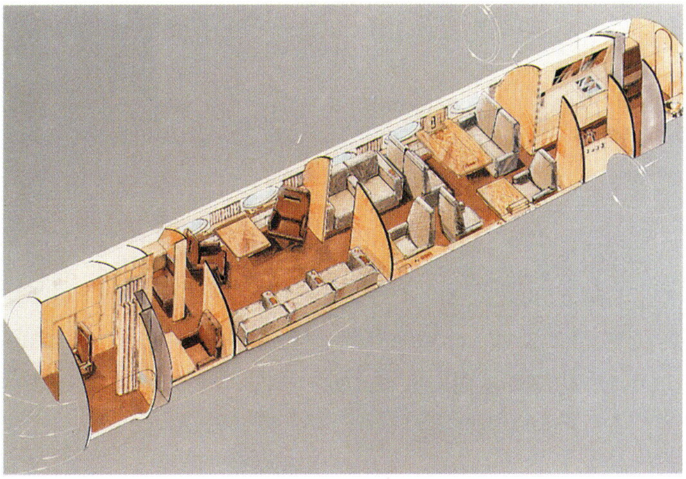

An artist's sketch of the inside of the VC-20 accomodations. (USAF Drawing)

Boeing VC-32A 757-200

In 1996, the Air Force announced the selction of the Boeing 757-200 as the replacement aircraft for the existing VC-137 fleet. The new aircraft are designated the VC-32A, with four planes ordered, and a mission of providing executive and congressional airlift support. On February 12, 1998, the first flight test was accomplished.

The first two C-32As entered operational service in June 1998, with the following two coming on board the following year. Like the previous VC-137s, the planes are operated by the 89th. The Air Force purchased the planes quite similarly to the way any commercial customer would buy a 757.

The C-32As are certified to the most-current FAA standards. Safety features on the aircraft include a Flight Management System (FMS) with an integrated, non-precision approach capable Global Positioning System (GPS), windshear warning integrated with the Ground Proximity Warning System (GPWS), Traffic Alert and Collision Avoidance Systems (TCAS), and the most capable flight data and voice recorders available.

The planes were designed to carry at least 45 passengers, a 16 person crew, and associated baggage non-stop from Frankfort, Germany, to Andrews Air Force Base at normal cruise speed.

Other Presidential Support Aircraft

During the 1960s, there were several pure-piston transports that supported VIP and presidential operations. These included a number of Lockheed VC-121 Super Constellations and Douglas VC-118s, which were basically DC-6s.

Although not officially a member of the presidential fleet, there have been other aircraft through the years that were used to support the mission when Air Force One was in the air.

Earlier, a modified KC-135 tanker went along on many presidential trips. The Stratotanker was crammed with elec-

This Marine Sikorsky VH-34C, 57-1684, had a long tenure of presidential service. (PASM Photo)

President Eisenhower boards VH-34C in October 1958 at Camp David. (Eisenhower Libary via Pima Air and Space Museum)

President Eisenhower, with grandson David, walk away from their VC-34C in Washington, D.C., in 1960. (Eisenhower Library via Pima Air and Space Museum)

A VH-3D Sea King helicopter of Marine Squadron 1 (HMX-1) takes off for Camp David from the White House in 1981. (USMC Photo)

tronic equipment which allowed it to serve as an airborne command post.

Also, during the 1960s, there was a so-called "Talking Bird" aircraft that went along on certain presidential missions. One of these planes was a modified C-97 Stratofreighter that carried a complete radio station and 18 communications specialists. It also carried a sideband transceiver among its equipment.

During the Kennedy era, there was an interesting sidelight when a Kennedy family aircraft, a Convair 240 that carried the name Caroline. Although the president had flown in the craft before being elected, but probably not after being inaugurated, it was a not considered to be a part of the official presidential fleet.

Marines assigned to Marine Helicopter Squadron i(HMX-1) usher a presidential aide aboard a VH-1N Iroquois helicopter at the conclusion of the 1988 Venice Summit. President Reagan will be boarding the helicopter shortly. (USMC Photo)

With those famous white columns of the White House in the background, a VH-3D takes to the air. (USMC Photo)

Former President Reagan and wife walk from Marine One at Andrews Air Force Base prior to boarding the VC-137 Air Force One. (USMC Photo)

President George Bush and Barbara Bush are transported by limousine to Marine One VH-60D Night Hawk in 1992. (USMC Photo)

The Air Force used Bell UH-13J Sioux helicopters like this one to support presidential transportation requirements. (Bill Holder Photo)

Marine Corps One, a VH-60N helicopter from the Executive Flight Detachment of Marine Helicopter Squadron One, Quantico, Virginia, waits to transport the president. (USMC Photo)

A view of a presidential VC-32A under construction at the Boeing Wichita Kansas facility. (Boeing Photo)

Two of the four C-32As on the ramp at Boeing Wichita. (Boeing Photo)

The last of four C-32As made its first flight November 5, 1998. (Boeing Photo)